WORDS TO RIDE BY

WORDS TO RIDE BY

Thoughts on Bicycling

MICHAEL CARABETTA

CHRONICLE BOOKS

SAN FRANCISCO

Dedicated to Bill Cunningham

1929–2016

wheelman, lensman, gentleman

Compilation copyright © 2017 by
Chronicle Books LLC

Library of Congress Cataloging-in-
Publication Data available.

ISBN: 978-1-4521-4536-5

Pages 110–112 constitute a
continuation of the copyright
page.

Manufactured in China
Designed by Hillary Caudle

Front cover: Henry Miller on a
bicycle in Santa Monica, California,
1975. Photograph by Peter
Gowland.
Back cover: Albert Einstein,
in a letter to his son Eduard,
February 5, 1930.

Picture editor: Julien Tomasello
Quotation research: Dean Burrell

MIX
Paper from
responsible sources
FSC™ C012521

10 9 8 7 6 5 4 3

Chronicle Books LLC
680 Second Street
San Francisco, California 94107
www.chroniclebooks.com

Introduction

I don't think I truly began to ride, or understand what it means to ride, until I weaned myself off my knobby-tired mountain bike and discovered the pleasure of a road bike—skinny tires and all.

As most kids do, I rode round the neighborhood on a cruiser. Many years later, in the flush of the 10-speed craze, I graduated to a French-made model. I even smoked the occasional Gauloises.

A move to Marin County, California, birthplace of the mountain bike, kindled my interest in this new form of cycling. Cobbled together with old Schwinn cruiser frames, motocross-style handlebars, and gears borrowed from road bikes, these "klunkers" (as they were called) signaled a new era in the evolution of the bicycle. Once they were manufactured, I was not alone in wanting one, and the fat tire bike became my ride of choice as I traversed the fire roads and trails on Mt. Tamalpais following in the tracks of the sport's innovators.

But after some time enduring the gnarly trails, grunt-inducing climbs, and whiplash drops, I found I preferred road biking like a smooth alto sax solo to mountain biking's shredding guitar riffs. Roads are graded, the ascents less grueling, the descents less wicked, the turns flowing. That was it for me—the flow. I could think about the ride: the cadence, the rhythm, the visceral connection between me, the bike, and the road.

I ride my bike to work, a round trip commute of about twelve miles per day, and aim for longer rides of twenty to twenty-five miles on the weekends, up to 50 when I can. On longer weekend rides I have a regular riding partner. And while I don't generally bike with a group, I like the romance of the French word for a group of cyclists, *peloton*, and I do feel part of the greater community of riders.

As cyclists know, the longer the ride, the more your thoughts can range. Call it a form of meditation. The commutes are shorter and so thoughts of the day ahead crowd in. But on longer rides, it's as if you're in a moving landscape streaming by. You notice things you don't notice if you're driving. I'll see things like the first appearance of lupine on a hillside, or wild irises opening up, and occasionally the gurgling brook. The mind may turn up philosophical questions, like what matters to me and why? Or *why am I turning these pedals over and over?*

Working as I do in publishing, I noticed that ever since Lance Armstrong's *It's Not About the Bike* (and Robert Penn's answering title, *It's All About the Bike*) there has been a small but growing number of cycling books published that go beyond practical and performance concerns to more thoughtful works on bikes and biking. These include meditations such as David Byrne's *Bicycle Diaries* and Paul Fournel's *Need for the Bike* as well as fiction such as Tim Krabbé's *The Rider*, a first person narrative of a one-day classic race. They feel like spiritual heirs to Henry Miller's classic *My Bike & Other Friends*.

Because much of what I do (and studied) is visual, I envisioned a book that might bring together the philosophic and kinetic aspects of bicycle and bicycling, quotations and visuals, which might capture some of the sensations cyclists feel when riding. The deeper I dug, the more I discovered—a motherlode of evocative, insightful, and sometimes funny words and images: men and women of letters and science, feted athletes, actors, musicians, and anonymous riders; smiles, grimaces, aches, antics, and the reflections of the riders lost in the experience. In sharing this collection of thoughts and images, it's my hope you might that discover—or rediscover—the essence of what the bike is all about.

—Michael Carabetta

Michael Carabetta is an award-winning creative director, designer, and avid cyclist. He lives and rides in the San Francisco Bay Area.

The Bicycle is a curious vehicle.
Its passenger is its engine.

JOHN HOWARD

When man invented the bicycle he reached the peak of his attainments. Here was a machine of precision and balance for the convenience of man. . . . Progress should have stopped when man invented the bicycle.

ELIZABETH HOWARD WEST

Parts diagram from the book, Ma petite bicyclette: Son anatomie, *by Charles-Louis Baudry de Saunier, 1925.*

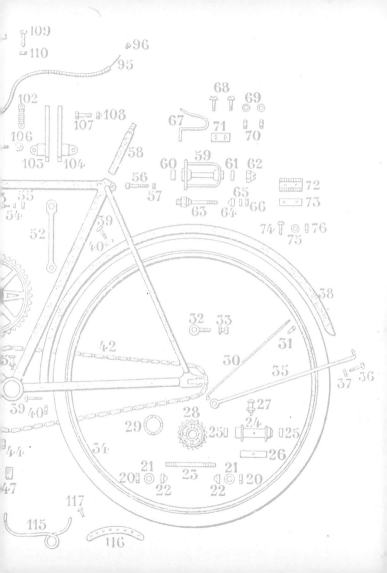

The bicycle, the bicycle surely, should always be the vehicle of novelists and poets.

Novelist and travel writer Bruce Chatwin on his bicycle, Fishers Island, New York circa 1975.

Smile
at miles!

Rollfast BICYCLES

Since 1895

Streamlined beauty of American design & craftsmanship

D. P. HARRIS HDW. & MFG. COMPANY, Inc.
ROLLFAST BUILDING, NEW YORK, N. Y.
BICYCLES · CUB-CYCLES · PLAYCYCLES · TRI-BIKES · ROLLER SKATES

When I go biking, I repeat a mantra of the day's sensations: bright sun, blue sky, warm breeze, blue jay's call, ice melting and so on. This helps me transcend the traffic, ignore the clamorings of work, leave all the mind theaters behind and focus on nature instead.

DIANE ACKERMAN

A 1946 print ad for Rollfast Bicycles.

It is by riding a bicycle that you learn the contours of a country best, since you have to sweat up the hills and can coast down them.

ERNEST HEMINGWAY

Cyclists on the access road to the lighthouse at Cap de Formentor, Mallorca, Balearic Islands, Spain.

The first real grip I ever got on things is when I learned the art of pedaling.

SEAMUS HEANEY

Actor Peter O'Toole as Dr. Harry Wolper in the film Creator *, 1985.*

When the spirits are low, when the day appears dark, when work becomes monotonous, when hope hardly seems worth having, just mount a bicycle and go out for a spin down the road, without thought on anything but the ride you are taking.

SIR ARTHUR CONAN DOYLE

British cyclist Eileen Sheridan, circa 1953.

Plenty of speed — no thought of danger.

A bicycle does get you there and more. . . . And there is always the thin edge of danger to keep you alert and comfortably apprehensive. Dogs become dogs again and snap at your raincoat; potholes become personal. And getting there is all the fun.

BILL EMERSON

Illustration from The "Don'ts" of Bicycling, *a 1969 manual from the Police and Sheriffs Safety Council, Santa Barbara, California.*

From left: Charmian Carr, Duane Chase, Debbie Turner, Julie Andrews, Angela Cartwright, and Nicholas Hammond in a scene from The Sound of Music, 1965.

24

Melancholy is
incompatible with
bicycling.

JAMES E. STARRS

The bicycle is just as good company as most husbands and, when it gets old and shabby, a woman can dispose of it and get a new one without shocking the entire community.

ANN STRONG

Illustration of a lady's safety bicycle, 1889.

If I can bicycle, I bicycle.

SIR DAVID ATTENBOROUGH

A participant in the 1957 Velodrome d'Hiver (six-day bicycle race) in Paris takes a tea and newspaper break. Photograph by Henri Cartier-Bresson.

Good morale in cycling comes
from good legs.

SEAN YATES

COPYRIGHT
VANNORMAN.
PHOTO.
SPRINGFIELD.

ORIENT

Four men on the Orient Quad bicycle, photo circa 1898.

Why should anyone steal a watch when he can steal a bicycle?

FLANN O'BRIEN

Film still from Ladri Di Biciclette (Bicycle Thieves), 1948.

Let me tell you what I think of bicycling. I think it has done more to emancipate women than anything else in the world. It gives women a feeling of freedom and self-reliance. I stand and rejoice every time I see a woman ride by on a wheel . . . the picture of free, untrammeled womanhood.

SUSAN B. ANTHONY

Three women with a bicycle, England, 1895.

So perfect is the safety bicycle, in fact, that, if the rider had sufficient skill not to interfere with its action, it will travel straight ahead and keep its own balance.

E.J. PRINDLE,
Scientific American, 1896

Photograph by Heidi Swift.

. . . [T]hings look different from the seat of a bike carrying a sleeping bag with a cold beer tucked inside.

JIM MALUSA

A 2009 campaign photograph for Mission Workshop's Mission Workshop Pack.

If the constellations had been named in the twentieth century, I suppose we would see bicycles . . .

CARL SAGAN

A still from E.T., 1982.

41

Bicycling is a big part of the future. It has to be. There's something wrong with a society that drives a car to work out in a gym.

BILL NYE THE SCIENCE GUY

Illustration by Joe Dator.

You're moving through a wonderful natural environment and working on balance, timing, depth perception, judgment . . . It forms kind of a ballet.

CHARLIE CUNNINGHAM

English bicycle polo, 1935.

Think of bicycles as rideable art that can just about save the world.

GRANT PETERSEN

An 1886 advertisment for Columbia Bicycles crafted by the Pope Manufacturing Company.

The bicycle ran with special ease at dusk, the tire emitting a kind of whisper as it palpated each rise and dip in the hard earth along the edge of the road.

VLADIMIR NABOKOV

A circle of sun highlights people riding their bicycles in Ferrara, Italy.
Photograph by William Albert.

It was a fact I've always wanted a bike. Speed gave me a thrill.

ALAN SILLITOE

When I see an adult on a bicycle, I do not despair for the future of the human race.

H.G. WELLS

Butch Cassidy (Paul Newman) on bicycle to the delight of Etta Place (Katherine Ross) in a scene from Butch Cassidy and the Sundance Kid, *1969.*

You want to be like a carpet unrolling. Get faster as the climb goes on.

CHRIS CARMICHAEL

Photograph by Gruber Images.

I was not yet sixteen when I understood a great deal, from having ridden bicycles for so long, about style, speed, grace, purpose, value, form, integrity, health, humor, music, breathing, and finally and perhaps best, of the relationship between the beginning and the end.

WILLIAM SAROYAN

Teenagers in Torino, Italy, circa 1950.

I learned the old school of cycling, where the more it hurts, the better.

JÖRG MÜLLER

Cyclist Eddie Triest, with partner, showing results of injuries as he competes in a six-day velodrome at Chicago Stadium, 1935.

We each carry our
own Tour de France
inside us.

PHILIPPE BRUNEL

Photograph by Ryan Siu.

Fig. 1

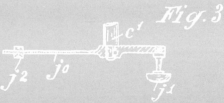

Fig. 3

Of all sports, cycling is the one that requires the most perfect match of man and machine. The more perfect the match, the more perfect the result.

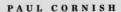

PAUL CORNISH

The first patented design of a prone-lying bicycle by M. Louis Hubault, 1934.

A photograph from the book Dr. Neesen's Book on Wheeling, *an 1899 physician's guide to the popular activity.*

Next to a leisurely walk I enjoy a "spin" on my tandem bicycle. It is splendid to feel the wind blowing in my face and the springy motion of my iron steed. The rapid rush through the air gives me a delicious sense of strength and buoyancy, and the exercise makes my pulses dance and my heart sing.

HELEN KELLER

Life is like riding a bicycle.
To keep your balance you
must keep moving.

ALBERT EINSTEIN

*Albert Einstein riding a bicycle in front of Ben Meyer's
house in Santa Barbara, California, 1933.*

He dropped down the hills on his bicycle. The roads were greasy, so he had to let it go. He felt a pleasure as the machine plunged over the second, steeper drop in the hill . . . His bicycle seemed to fall beneath him, and he loved it.

D.H. LAWRENCE

Photograph by Moodboard.

I won! I won! I don't have to go to school anymore.

EDDY MERCKX,
after winning his first bicycle race

Eddy Merckx, winner of the Giro d'Italia on the podium, 1968.

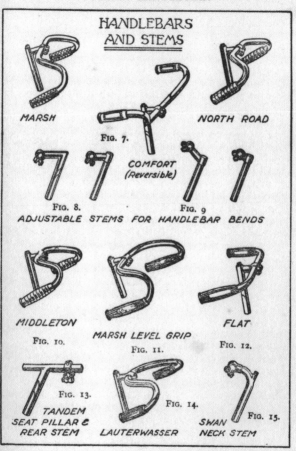

HANDLEBARS
AND STEMS

MARSH

FIG. 7.

COMFORT
(Reversible)

NORTH ROAD

FIG. 8.

FIG. 9.

ADJUSTABLE STEMS FOR HANDLEBAR BENDS

MIDDLETON

FIG. 10.

MARSH LEVEL GRIP

FIG. 11.

FLAT

FIG. 12.

FIG. 13.

TANDEM
SEAT PILLAR &
REAR STEM

FIG. 14.

LAUTERWASSER

SWAN
NECK STEM

FIG. 15.

FIGS. 7 to 15.—Various types of handlebars and stems.

The world lies right beyond the handlebars of any bicycle that I happen to be on anywhere from New York Bay to the Vallée de Chevreuse.

DANIEL BEHRMAN

Illustration depicting various types of handlebars and stems reprinted from Every Cyclist's Handbook *by F.J. Camm, 1936.*

There are three ways to pedal a bike. With the legs, with the lungs, or with the heart.

MANDIBLE JONES

Britt (Gloucester, MA), *September 2012; Silver gelatin print by Keith Snyder.*

Dairy Queen. God, I dream about Dairy Queens.

GREG LEMOND,
when asked what he thinks about during races in Europe

Dairy Queen sign in Verona, Pennsylvania. Photograph by Debra Jane Seltzer.

ILLUSTRATION OF LIGHT ROADSTER MACHINE, BUILT ENTIRELY OF B.S.A. FITTINGS

NOTE.—The Company do not supply Complete Machines.

The essence of bicycling is the beauty of the machine itself. The technical simplicity, the light weight, the slowly advancing trick components—that's absolutely as much of the beauty and joy of cycling as the fact that the guy on the bike happens to be a physical machine with muscles.

JACK LAMBIE

Illustration of Light Roadster Machine from the 1903 Birmingham Small Arms Company catalog.

Cycling in general, and racing in particular, has a way of ordering and fulfilling our lives. When we get into cycling, we inherit a point of view, a perception, an attitude toward life.

OWEN MULHOLLAND

Cyclist John Bange riding the "Azure Star" on a dirt track at Aviadell near Clifton Queensland, Australia, circa 1930.

Get a bicycle. You will not regret it, if you live.

MARK TWAIN

Actor Steve McQueen photographed on set during the making of the film Le Mans; Le Mans, France 1970. Photograph by Raymond Depardon.

An invitation to the undertaker.

The very existence of the bicycle is an offense to reason and wisdom.

P.J. O'ROURKE

Illustration from The "Don'ts" of Bicycling, *a 1969 manual from the Police and Sheriffs Safety Council, Santa Barbara, California.*

As a kid I had a dream—I wanted to own my own bicycle. When I got the bike I must have been the happiest boy in Liverpool, maybe the world. I lived for that bike. Most kids left their bike in the backyard at night. Not me. I insisted on taking mine indoors and the first night I even kept it in my bed.

JOHN LENNON

John Lennon photographed riding a bicycle on the Magical Mystical Tour *set, 1967.*

It's not about the bike.

LANCE ARMSTRONG

An illustration accompanying an advertisement for the Corbin Duplex Model 8 Coaster Brake appearing in a 1919 issue of American Boy *magazine.*

Most bicyclists in New York City obey instinct far more than they obey the traffic laws, which is to say that they run red lights, go the wrong way on one-way streets, violate cross-walks, and terrify innocents, because it just seems easier that way. Cycling in the city, and particularly in midtown, is anarchy without malice.

AUTHOR UNKNOWN,
from *The New Yorker* "Talk of the Town,"
June 9, 1986

Bike messenger in New York City.

"On your left."

Bike riding as little as three miles a day will improve your sex life.

DR. FRANCO ANTONINI

Illustration by Michael Crawford.

I took care of my wheel as one would look after a Rolls Royce. If it needed repairs I always brought it to the same shop. . . . Often he would do a job for me without pay, because, as he put it, he never saw a man so in love with his bike as I was.

HENRY MILLER

Henry Miller on a bicycle in Santa Monica, California, 1975.
Photograph by Peter Gowland.

To me, cycling is the joy of the wind in your face, the sound of the tyres on the road and the feeling of freedom.

SIR PAUL SMITH

An early portrait of Paul Smith.

It is the unknown around the corner that turns my wheels.

HEINZ STÜCKE

A 1948 advertisement for Ferodo all-weather bicycle brakes, illustrated by Frank Patterson.

Let our people travel light and free on their bicycles.

EDWARD ABBEY

Photograph by Matthew Wiebe.

Romance is when they will wait for you at the top of the hill.

ALICE B. TOECLIPS,

sometimes known as Jacquie Phelan

Julie Vicks and Martin Paviet, 2015. Photograph by James Startt.

Anyone who rides a bike is a friend of mine.

GARY FISHER

*New bicycle helps solve transit problem;
undated photograph from the U.S. Library of Congress.*

[V]ariable gears are only for people over forty-five. Isn't it better to triumph by the strength of your muscles rather than by the artifice of a derailleur? We are getting soft. . . . As for me, give me a fixed gear.

HENRI DESGRANGE

Johnson S. Johnson, the first person to bicycle one mile in less than two minutes, from Spalding's Official Bicycle Guide for 1898.

Ever bike? Now that's something that makes life worth living! . . . And then go home again after three hours of it . . . and then to think that tomorrow I can do it all over again!

JACK LONDON

Photograph by Jonas Kullman.

TEXT SOURCES

8: Howard, John. *The Cyclist's Companion*. New York: Penguin Books, 1984. **10:** West, Elizabeth. *Hovel in the Hills: An Account of the "Simple Life."* London: Faber & Faber, 1977. **13:** Morley, Christopher. *Parnassus on Wheels*. New York: Doubleday, Page & Co., 1917. **15:** Ackerman, Diane. *Deep Play*. New York: Random House, 1999. **16:** Hemingway, Ernest. From *By-Line, Ernest Hemingway: Selected Articles and Dispatches of Four Decades by Ernest Hemingway*, edited by William White. New York: Charles Scribner's Sons, 1967. **19:** Heaney, Seamus. From "Wheels within Wheels." *Seeing Things*. New York: Farrar, Straus and Giroux, 1993. **21:** Doyle, Sir Arthur Conan, "Dr. Conan Doyle on Cycling." *Scientific American*, August 22, 1896. **23:** Emerson, Bill, "On Bicycling." *Saturday Evening Post*, July 29, 1967. **25:** Starrs, James E., ed. *The Literary Cyclist*. New York: Breakaway Books, 1997. Originally published under the title *The Noiseless Tenor* (New York and London: Cornwall Books, 1982). **27:** Strong, Ann. *Minneapolis Tribune*, 1895. **29:** Attenborough, David. From inspirationalstories.com, accessed July 1, 2016, http://www.inspirationalstories .com/quotes/t/david-attenborough/. **30:** Burke, Edmund R. *Serious Cycling, 2nd Edition*. Champaign, IL: Human Kinetics, 2002. **32:** O'Brien, Flann. *The Third Policeman*. Dublin, Ireland: Dalkey Archive Press, 1967. **35:** Anthony, Susan B. From "Champion of Her Sex: Miss Susan B. Anthony," interview by Nellie Bly. *New York World*, 2 February 1896. **37:** Prindle, E. J. "Riding a Bicycle Backward." *Scientific American*. May 13, 1899. **39:** Malusa, Jim. *Into Thick Air: Biking to the Bellybutton of Six Continents*. San Francisco: Sierra Club Books, 2008. **41:** Sagan, Carl. *Cosmos*. New York: Random House, 1980. **43:** Nye, Bill. From *Cancer: 101 Solutions to a Preventable Epidemic*, by Liz Armstrong, Guy Dauncey, and Anne Wordsworth. Gabriola, British Columbia: New Society Publishers, 2007. **45:** Cunningham, Charlie, "No Happy Trails When Cyclists, Bikers Share." *Moscow-Pullman Daily News*. April 16, 1993. Pullman, WA/Moscow, ID. Vol. 81, no. 171. **47:** Petersen, Grant. From *Bike Porn, Vol. 1*, edited by Chris Naylor. West Sussex, England: Summersdale Publishers Ltd., 2013. **49:** Nabokov, Vladimir. *Mary*. New York: McGraw-Hill Book Company, 1970. **51:** Sillitoe, Alan. "The Bike." First published in *The Ragman's Daughter and Other Stories*. London: Allen, 1963; New York: Knopf, 1964. **53:** Wells, H. G. *The Wheels of Chance*. London: J. M. Dent & Co., 1896. **55:** Carmichael, Chris. From "Bike Bits" bulletin. *Adventure Cyclist 9* (September 5, 2007), no.17. **57:** Saroyan, William. *The Bicycle Rider in Beverly Hills*. New York: Ballantine Books, 1952. **59:** Müller, Jörg. From *The Quotable Cyclist: Great Moments of Bicycling Wisdom, Inspiration and Humor*, edited by Bill Strickland. Halcottsville, NY: Breakaway Books, 2001. **61:** Brunel, Philippe. *An Intimate Portrait of the Tour de France: Masters and Slaves of the Road*. Denver, CO: Buonpane Publications, 1996. **63:** Cornish, Paul. From *Cycling*

Fast: Winning Essentials for Cycling Competition, by Robert Panzera. Champaign, IL: Human Kinetics. 2010. **65:** Keller, Helen. *The Story of My Life.* 1903. **67:** Einstein, Albert. Letter to his son Eduard, February 5, 1930. **68:** Lawrence, D. H. *Sons and Lovers.* London: Gerald Duckworth and Company Ltd., 1913. **71:** Merckx, Eddy. From Bicycle Kingdom, accessed July 1, 2016, http://www.bicyclekingdom.com/bikes/quotes/cycling_1.htm. **73:** Behrman, Daniel. *The Man Who Loved Bicycles: The Memoirs of an Autophobe.* New York: Harper's Magazine Press, 1973. **75:** Jones, Mandible. From *The Quotable Cyclist: Great Moments of Bicycling Wisdom, Inspiration and Humor,* edited by Bill Strickland. Halcottsville, NY: Breakaway Books, 2001. **77:** LeMond, Greg. From *Sports Nutrition for Endurance Athletes* (2nd edition), by Monique Ryan. Boulder, CO: Velo Press, 2007. **79:** Lambie, Jack. From *The Quotable Cyclist: Great Moments of Bicycling Wisdom, Inspiration and Humor,* edited by Bill Strickland. Halcottsville, NY: Breakaway Books, 2001. **81:** Mulholland, Owen. From *The Bicycling Big Book of Training: Everything You Need to Know to Take Your Riding to the Next Level,* edited by Danielle Kosecki. Emmaus, PA: Rodale Books, 2015. **83:** Twain, Mark. "Taming the Bicycle" (essay). 1893. **85:** O'Rourke, P. J. "A Cool and Logical Analysis of the Bicycle Menace." From *Republican Party Reptile : The Confessions, Adventures, Essays, and (Other) Outrages of. . . .* New York: Atlantic Monthly Press, 1987. **87:** Lennon, John. From *Cycling's Strangest Tales: Extraordinary but True Stories,* by Iain Spragg. London: Pavilion Books, 2014. **89:** Armstrong, Lance. *It's Not about the Bike: My Journey Back to Life.* New York: Putnam, 2000. **90:** Author unknown. From "Talk of the Town." *The New Yorker,* June 9, 1986. **93:** Antonini, Franco. From *Keep Calm and Pedal On,* edited by Elaine Scott. London: Ebury Press. 2015. **94:** Miller, Henry. *My Bike & Other Friends.* Santa Barbara: Capra Press, 1978. **97:** Smith, Paul. Quotation in correspondence with the author, 2016. **99:** Stücke, Heinz. From *Bike Porn, Vol. 1,* edited by Chris Naylor. West Sussex, England: Summersdale Publishers Ltd., 2013. **101:** Abbey, Edward. *Desert Solitaire.* New York: McGraw-Hill Education, 1968. **103:** Phelan, Jacquie. Quotation in correspondence with the author, 2016. **105:** Fisher, Gary. From twitter.com, accessed July 1, 2016, https://twitter.com/gary_fisher/status/556876661635837953. **107:** Desgrange, Henri. From *Bike Mechanic: How to Be an Ace Bike Mechanic (Instant Expert),* by Paul Mason. Mankato, MN: Capstone Press, 2011. **108:** London, Jack. *The Letters of Jack London: Volume One: 1896-1905,* edited by Earle Labor, Robert C. Leitz III, and I. Milo Shepard. Stanford, CA: Stanford University Press, 1988.